Earth Afire with God

CELTIC PRAYERS FOR ORDINARY LIFE

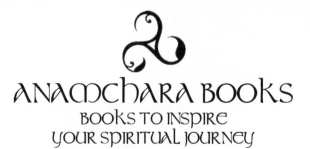

ΑΝΑΟΟΧΗΑRΑ BOOKS
BOOKS TO INSPIRE
YOUR SPIRITUAL JOURNEY

In Celtic Christianity, an *anamchara* is a soul friend, a companion and mentor (often across the miles and the years) on the spiritual journey. Soul friendship entails a commitment to both accept and challenge, to reach across all divisions in a search for the wisdom and truth at the heart of our lives.

At Anamchara Books, we are committed to creating a community of soul friends by publishing books that lead us into deeper relationships with God, the Earth, and each other. These books connect us with the great mystics of the past, as well as with more modern spiritual thinkers. They are designed to build bridges, shaping an inclusive spirituality where we all can grow.

You can order our books at **www.AnamcharaBooks.com**. Check out our site to read opinions and perspectives from our editorial staff on our Soul Friends blog. You can also submit your own blog posts by emailing **info@AnamcharaBooks.com** with "Blog Entry for Soul Friends" in the subject line. To find out more about Anamchara Books and connect with others on their own spiritual journeys, visit **www.AnamcharaBooks.com** today.

ΑΝΑΟΟΧΗΑRΑ BOOKS
220 Front Street
Vestal, New York 13850
(607) 785-1578
www.AnamcharaBooks.com

Earth Afire with God

CELTIC PRAYERS FOR ORDINARY LIFE

Anamchara Books

Anamchara Books

Vestal, NY 13850

First Printing

9 8 7 6 5 4 3 2 1

IngramSpark 2020 paperback ISBN: 978-1-62524-799-5

Library of Congress Control Number: 2011902459

Interior and cover design by MK Bassett-Harvey.
Edited by the staff at Anamchara Books.
Printed in the United States of America.

Contents

Introduction

"Earth's crammed with heaven, And every common bush afire with God," wrote Elizabeth Barrett Browning. In other words, the world where we live is sacred. If we pay attention, our physical senses are capable of perceiving the Holy all around us. Each glimpse we have of the Earth, each sound we hear, and every bite of food we eat can reveal to us the deeper dimension in which we live our lives. Even our most ordinary routines are filled with God.

But all too often, we miss these everyday revelations. Our culture directs our attention elsewhere. We live our lives focused on our to-do lists, preoccupied with what's coming up next, rather than being truly present in the ordinary reality of the right-now. We often set boundaries in time and space around our "holy times," restricting them to Sunday mornings inside a church.

But the ancient Celtic Christians put no boundaries around holiness. They saw the Divine hand at work in the cycles of the natural world, in day and night, birth and death, as well as the turning wheel of the seasons. They affirmed that God was present not only in the beauties of Nature, but also in the most ordinary moments: getting up in the morning, washing, working, eating, going to bed.

And they also knew the power of the spoken word. By putting their awareness of God's presence into prayers, they blessed both their lives and themselves. They shaped their consciousness; they taught themselves to be ever more sensitive to this world's glimpses of heaven.

These spoken prayers were handed down from parents to children, a rich heritage of blessing that gave each new generation the awareness of God's hands touching their lives. The traditional Celtic way of life has all but disappeared, but many of these ancient prayers were recorded and compiled in the late nineteenth and early twentieth centuries. Most of the prayers included in this book are based on prayers from these compilations.

In many ways, of course, the world where those long-ago Celts lived was far different from the world where most of us live today. Theirs was a world where time was marked by the rhythms of seedtime and harvest, by the solstices and equinoxes, by the tides and the lambing of ewes. They had no televisions or computers, no electric lights or central heating to distract their attention from the natural world's cycles. The daily demands of their lives kept them close to the Earth.

And yet we can learn from their example. We too can bless our daily lives with the same words they used. We can infuse the every-day with an awareness of God's imminent presence in all things, seen and unseen. To that end, Anamchara Books has updated many of these ancient prayers so that they encompass the realities of twenty-first-century life. We've written a few of our own as well. (Notes at the back of this book identify the sources of each prayer.) We're confident that the same Spirit who blew a holy wind through the Celts' agricultural year still breathes through today's Internet and car trips, through office work and even the television.

These Celtic prayers reveal a friendly world that's sanctified by daily intimate expressions of love between God and humans. We see this in a conversation recorded in Alexander Carmichael's *Carmina Gadelica* (one of the nineteenth-century sources we used), where a woman named Catherine Maclennan describes the habits of praise and blessing she learned as a child:

> My mother would be asking us to sing our morning song to God down in the back-house, as Mary's lark was singing it up in the clouds, and as Christ's mavis [song thrush] was singing it yonder in the tree, giving glory to the God of the creatures for the repose of the night, for the light of the day, and for the joy of life. She would tell us that every creature on the earth here below and in the ocean beneath and in the air above was giving glory to the great God of the creatures and the worlds, of the virtues and the blessings, [so why would] we be dumb! My dear mother reared her children in food and clothing, in love and charity.

The Celts saw not only God in the world around them but the entire Divine family as well: Mary, the apostles, angels, and holy men and women who had gone before them. The communion of saints was a lived reality for Celtic Christians, one that was interwoven through the natural world.

The angel Michael was one of their favorites. Traditionally, Michael represents divine strength and courage in the face of evil, and the Celtic Christians were especially aware of Michael as one who dwells in the midst of the sea and wind. In the Celtic lands of Ireland, Scotland, Wales, Cornwall, and Brittany, many high places were dedicated to him. For the Celts, Michael represented the holy energy that gives itself on behalf of others, that risks all for the sake of love. The Celtic people believed that Creation is good, filled with God's own goodness, but they also knew that evil is in the world. They called on Michael as a defender of body and soul against the forces of evil. He was particularly invoked for protection on journeys, including death's final journey. As an angel of God, he rides the winds of God's creative goodness, serving the living Christ. He walks with us from the beginning of our lives all the way through to the end, where he guides us to eternity.

Brigid (also known as Bride) was another beloved saint of the Celtic Christians. The ancient Celtic goddess with the same name was the goddess of the hearth fire (including pregnancy, childbirth, family, and healing), the patroness of creative crafts (such as fabric arts and metalwork), and the muse of poetry and knowledge. Saint Brigid of Kildare, an actual woman who lived in the fifth century, seems to have been in many ways the Christian incarnation of this pagan goddess. The Celtic church loved to tell stories about Saint Brigid's ample generosity: if she gave a drink of water to a thirsty stranger, the liquid turned into milk; when she sent a barrel of beer to a Christian community, it proved to satisfy seventeen more; she changed her bath water into beer to quench the thirst of an unexpected guest; and even her cows gave milk three times the same day to provide milk for visitors. Brigid was also one of the many Celtic saints who insisted that having a soul friend (*anamchara*) is a vital component of the spiritual life—and after her death, she continued to be a soul friend to all who called on her.

Michael and Brigid, along with other Gaelic saints like Patrick and Columba, may seem irrelevant to our modern world. But here at Anamchara Books, we believe they can still enrich our lives, teaching us to appreciate the Earth-centered, incarnational Christianity that is at the heart of the Celtic way. Often when we take a look at our lives from a new and unfamiliar angle, we see more than we ever did before. Our understanding is deepened, and our awareness of God expands.

"Attention is love," says poet Marge Piercy in her book *The Art of Blessing the Day: Poems with a Jewish Theme* (Knopf, 2000). "Bless whatever you can with eyes and hands and tongue." This sense of blessing is embedded in many world faiths, including Judaism and Hinduism, but it is often overlooked in modern Western Christianity. Too often we forget to pay attention to the everyday world around us. We fail to see . . . or touch . . . or speak the holiness of all that is.

The prayers we've included in this volume call us to pay attention. They reflect a world where Spirit and Earth, life and death, the ordinary and the mystical are united. They remind us of the holiness of the everyday, the real presence of God in Creation, and our connection with those believers who have gone before us. They reveal the ordinary Earth afire with God.

We hope you enjoy them as much as we do!

Praying

Coming to God

I am bending my knee
In the eye of the Father who created me,
In the eye of the Son who purchased me,
In the eye of the Spirit who cleansed me,
     In friendship and affection.
Through Your own Anointed One, O God,
Bestow upon us fullness in our need,
     Love toward God,
     The affection of God,
     The smile of God,
     The wisdom of God,
     The grace of God,
     The fear of God,
     And the will of God
To do in the world of the Three,
As angels and saints
Do in heaven;
     Each shade and light,
     Each day and night,
     Each time in kindness,
     Give us Your Spirit.

A Plea

God, listen to my prayer,
Bend to me Your ear,
Let my supplications and my prayers
Ascend to You upward,
Come, O King of Glory,
To protect me downward,
O King of life and mercy
With the aid of the Lamb.
O Son of Mary Virgin
To protect me with power,
O Son of the lovely Mary
Of purest fairest beauty.

Let It Be So

I pray to God the Creator, God the Child,
And to God the Holy Spirit,
Whose infinite greatness enfolds the world,
In Persons three and one,
In essence simple and triune,
Who ever-living lives.
Let it be so. Let it be so.

Jesus, Hear Me

O holy Jesus,
Gentle Friend,
Morning Star,
Midday Sun,
Bright Flame of Righteousness,
Life Everlasting and Eternity,
Fountain Ever-New, Ever-Living, Ever-Lasting,
Heart's Desire,
Son of the Creator, without mother in Heaven,
Son of Mary, without father on Earth,
True and loving Brother,
Hear me, I pray.

Prayer of Offering

Thanks be to You, Jesus Christ,
For the many gifts You have given me,
Each day and night, each sea and land,
Each weather fair, each calm, each wild.
I am giving You worship with my whole life,
I am giving You my "Yes!" with my whole power,
I am giving You praise with my whole mouth,
I am giving You honor with all I say.
I am giving You reverence with my whole understanding,

I am giving You offering with my whole thought,
I am giving You praise with my whole fervor,
I am giving You humility in the blood of the Lamb.
I am giving You love with my whole devotion,
I am on my knees with my whole desire.
I am giving You love with my whole heart,
I am giving You affection with my all my senses.
I am giving You my existence with my whole mind,
I am giving You my soul, O God of all gods.
My thought, my deed,
My word, my will,
My understanding, my intellect,
My way, my state.
And I am beseeching You
To keep me from ill,
To keep me from hurt.
To keep me from harm,
To keep me from misfortune.
To keep me from grief,
To keep me this night, this day,
In the nearness of Thy love.

A Prayer for God's Presence

I see no light inside this face, or these eyes

Looking back at me.

And yet You inspired this fragile thing; into this little portion

You breathed Your Spirit, oh Creator God.

But how quickly and how easily I tire.

Rescue me from vanity, and from self-loathing, too.

Put a light inside me, increase Your glory. Come, Spirit!

Brighten my eyes and lighten my step:

Come, Spirit!

Free my blood to beat calmly in my breast:

Come, Spirit!

Humble me and make me unafraid to face the world:

Come, Spirit!

Bring me back into union with You,

oh Unity in Trinity, Trinity in Unity,

I call out to you.

Teach me to pray.

Morning Prayers

God Be with Us

God be with us
On this Your day,
> Amen.

To us and with us,
On this Your day,
> Amen.

Anything that is evil in us,
Or that may witness against us,
Where we shall longest be
When we live with You in Heaven,
Illumine it to us,
Banish it from us,
Root it out of our hearts,
Ever, evermore, everlastingly.
> Ever, evermore, everlastingly.
>> Amen.

The Guiding Light of Eternity

O God, who brought me from the rest of last night
Into the joyous light of this day,
Bring me from the new light of this day
Into the guiding light of eternity.
　　Oh! from the new light of this day
　　Into the guiding light of eternity.

The First Word I Say

The first word I say
In the morning when I arise
May it be Your Name.
May that Name be the armor I wear.
I shall put on the protection of the Christ today.

Washing Your Face

I am bathing my face
In the mild rays of the sun,
As Mary washed Christ
In the rich milk of Egypt.

Sweetness be in my mouth,
Wisdom be in my speech,
The love the fair Mary gave her Son
May I see at the center of all life.

The love of Christ in my breast,
The form of Christ protecting me,
There is nothing in sea or on land
That can overcome the King of the Lord's Day.

The hand of Bride about my neck,
The hand of Mary about my head,
The hand of Michael washing me,
The hand of Christ saving me.

Getting Dressed

Creator God, clothe me in Your kindness.

Outside these bedroom walls the world is waiting, hungry

For what I cannot give it, for what I am not

Capable of giving. Anoint me instead

On each eye, to see myself new in this mirror.

And help me choose colors for myself befitting

A royal child of the Most High Protector, brother and sister

To the Lord Jesus Christ.

Like the favorite child of Jacob, wrap me

In bright colors, in warmth and loving-kindness, so that wherever

I go, whatever I wear

—Whether rich or threadbare—

I will keep Christ's love close.

Unity in Trinity, Trinity in Unity,

I call out to you.

Come I This Day

Come I this day to the Creator
Come I this day to the Child,
Come I to the Holy Spirit powerful;
Come I this day with God,
Come I this day with Christ,
Come I with the Spirit of kindly balm,
God, and Spirit, and Jesus,
From the crown of my head
To the soles of my feet;
Come I with my reputation,
Come I with my testimony,
Come I to You, Jesus—

    Jesus, shelter me.

The Day's Dedication

Thanks to You, God,
Who brought me from yesterday
To the beginning of today,
Everlasting joy
To earn for my soul
With good intent.
And for every gift of peace
You bestow on me,
My thoughts, my words,
My deeds, my desires
I dedicate to You.
I ask You,
I beg You,
To keep me from offence,
And to shield me today,
For the sake of Your wounds
With Your offering of grace.

Morning Blessing

This day is Your love-gift to me.

I take this dawn from Your hand.

Make me busy in Your service

Throughout the hours ahead,

But not so busy that I cannot sing!

And may the south wind blow its tenderness through my heart

So that I bear myself gently toward all.

And may the day's sunlight

Pass into my thoughts,

So that each shall be a picture of Your thought,

Noble and right.

Blessing the Day's Preparation

As I rise from my bed,

Bless me, bright Lord.

As I wash my flesh with water,

Cleanse my heart, sweet Savior.

As I clothe my body,

Dress me in Your love, gracious Creator.

May I go forth into the world,

Adorned with Your Spirit.

I Arise Today in Strength

I arise today
Through a mighty strength:
God's power to guide me,
God's might to uphold me,
God's eyes to watch over me;
God's ear to hear me,
God's word to give me speech,
God's hand to guard me,
God's way to lie before me,
God's shield to shelter me,
God's host to secure me.

The Home

Blessing for Hearth-Keepers

Brigid of the Mantle, encompass us.
Lady of the Lambs, protect us.
Keeper of the Hearth, kindle us.
Beneath your mantle, gather us.
And restore us to memory.

Mothers of our mother,
Foremothers strong,
Guide our hands in yours,
Remind us how
To kindle the hearth,
To keep it bright,
To preserve the flame.
Your hands upon ours,
Our hands within yours,
To kindle the light
Both day and night.

The Mantle of Brigid about us,
The Memory of Brigid within us,
The Protection of Brigid keeping us
From harm, from ignorance, from heartlessness.
This day and night,
From dawn till dark,
From dark till dawn.

Kindling the Fire

I will raise the hearth-fire
As Mary would.
The encirclement of Bride and of Mary
On the fire, and on the floor,
And on the household all.
Who are they on the bare floor?
John and Peter and Paul.
Who are they by my bed?
The lovely Bride and her Fosterling.
Who are those watching over my sleep?
The fair loving Mary and her Lamb.
Who is that so near to me?
The King of the sun, He himself it is.
Who is that at the back of my head?
The Son of Life without beginning, without time

Lighting the House

Lord, grant me, I pray in the name of Jesus,
Christ the Son, my God, that as I light my house's lamps,
My heart too may be lit with love that knows no fail.
May my home's light shine out into the darkness,
And may my life's light so also shine.
O Christ, kindle both my home's lights and my heart,
Savior most sweet, that they may shine
Continually for You,
Receiving perpetual light from the light perpetual
So that our darkness may be driven from us.

A Prayer of Welcome

O King of stars!
Whether my house be dark or bright,
Never shall it be closed against anyone,
For Christ did open His house for me.

If there be a guest in your house,
And you share not with him,
It is not only the guest who will do without
But Jesus, Mary's Son, as well.

Christ in My Home

When a stranger came to my door,
I put food on the table,
I poured drink in my best cups,
I played music for him to hear,
And in the sacred name of the Trinity,
He blessed me and my house,
My animals, my belongings, and my dear ones.
And I heard the lark the next morning, singing,

 "Often, often, often
Goes the Christ in a stranger's form."

Blessing on the Home

The Sacred Three
Our fortress be,
Encircling we
Who live within these walls.
Come and be round
Our hearth, our home.

Protect this family
And every sleeping thing
Within this house
From harm, from sin.
Your care's our peace
Through dark of night
Till light's release.

Working

Prayer for Starting the Work Day

Lord Jesus, who worked at lathe and plane,
    with hammer and with nails,
Bless and sanctify the tools I use this day.

Lord Jesus, who worked beside His earthly father, Joseph,
Bless and watch over me and those with whom I work this day.

Lord Jesus, who knew the cares and frustrations of toil,
    Bless my work.

Lord Jesus, who knew the rewards and satisfaction of toil,
    Bless my work.

Lord Jesus, whose gifts of talent and ability sustain my working life,
    Bless my work.

In strength and with confidence I begin my work today.
In strength and with confidence may I accomplish all I must do.
To the Glory of God my Creator, I dedicate this day.

Workplace Prayer

The job I do today, Christ does it too.

May my workplace be bright with His joy.

May the Trinity be pleased with each task I do,

    Creator, Child, and Spirit,

And may the bright angels hover 'round my desk—

    Dear presence—each hour of the day.

Let every e-mail I send go forth in truth and blessing.

May I speak only words of truth and blessing

    On the phone and to my colleagues.

May no dealing of this day

Give shame to the bright people of Heaven,

    The holy cloud that watches all.

May I not forget them, nor the stout Earth that gives me strength,

    Nor You, fair Lord.

Daily Life

Blessing After a Quarrel

Bride went out
One morning early,
With her two horses.
One broke its leg
With much ado.
But what was apart
She put together
Bone to bone,
Flesh to flesh,
Sinew to sinew,
Vein to vein.
As she healed that
May we heal this.

Hungry

I am empty, O God.
My body craves the food it needs.
My soul craves the food it needs.
My mind craves the food it needs.

A growling stomach,
Despair and loneliness,
Boredom and unrest.
These are the signs of my hunger.

Fill me, O my God.
Strengthen my body with bread and fruit.
Strengthen my soul with love and friendship.
Strengthen my mind with truth and conversation.

Let me not forget that others hunger too.
Let me not forget that body, soul, and mind must all be fed.
Let me not deny my hunger.

Give me the means to feed others, O God.
As Christ multiplied the bread and fish,
Multiply nourishment through me.
And let me nourish those around me.

Blessing Before a Meal

Be with me, O God, at the breaking of bread.
Be with me, O God, with each bite I take.
May no morsel I partake
Add to my soul's freight.

At the Market

I praise You God, for this abundance,
For this harvest of plenty
In green, red, and gold.
Bless, O Father, those whose hands picked these.
Bless, O Christ, those whose hands arranged these here.
Bless, O Spirit, those whose hands and mouths and bodies
Will be satisfied by their eating.

In Thanksgiving for a Good Meal

All Glory to you, Creator of the Universe,
Who has fed me so well today!

In the name of the Creator, whose love and goodness sustains me,
In the name of the Child, whose love and goodness sustains me,
In the name of the Spirit, whose love and goodness sustains me,

I offer thanksgiving for this good meal!

For the bounty of the Earth, and the good things it brings forth,
I sing Your praises!
For the savor of good food and the refreshment of good drink,
I sing Your praises!
For the great honor of sharing
Your pleasure in what You have made,

I sing Your praises!

May this good meal strengthen me to do Your will,
May it sustain me in Your service,
May the pleasure of it remind me of
Your ever-present love and goodness!

A Love Blessing

Bless my partner on this Earth,
For we are two, yet one,
And You, O true God, are One in Three.

You who made both the Earth and the Moon,
Who created the sound of river water
And the never-ending sigh of the sea,
Who made the word in the book
And the flame of the candle,
Who made the song both of the wren and the whale,
The beauty of winter and summer,
And the joys of both night and day,
You who know that in difference is sweetness,
Yet in unity we find You.
Give joy to our senses,
On nights dear and tender,
Shine in our love,
For we are two, yet one,
O true God, who is One, yet Three.

When I Am Tired

Put Your salve on my sight,
Put Your balm on my wounds,
Wrap Your linen robe around my skin,
O Healing Hand, O Son of the God of salvation.

O God of the weak,
O God of the lowly,
O God of the righteous,
O shield of homesteads.
You are calling me
With the voice of glory,
With the mouth of mercy
Of Your beloved Son,

O may I find rest everlasting
In the home of Your Trinity,
In the Paradise of Your Peace,
In the Sun-Garden of Your love.

When We Are Sick and Out of Sorts

Fair Jesus, You are the best medicine,

And your food is sweeter than all else.

Sustain and guide our bodies at every spot.

The knee that is stiff, O Healer, make pliant.

The heart that is hard make warm beneath Your wing.

The soul that is wandering from Your path,

Grasp its helm and guide it back to life.

Each thing that is amiss in us, put right.

Each thing that is hard soften with Your grace.

Each wound that is giving us pain,

O Best of Healers, make whole.

O God of the Internet

My hands upon the keyboard.
    Keep my eyes from evil.
The world is at my fingertips.
    Keep my thoughts from evil.
Untold wealth of knowledge.
    Keep my heart from evil.

O God of the Internet,
O Christ of the wireless networks,
O Spirit of the world of information,
Turn my eyes to You,
Fix my thoughts on You,
Attune my heart to You.

You are Ruler of the wild streams of information,
Of the chaos of images, both seemly and unseemly.
There is nothing You do not touch.
There is nothing beyond the reach of Your fingers.
There is nothing that cannot be redeemed by You.
Open my eyes, O God.
Show me Your truth in all I read.
Show me Your beauty in all I see.
Show me Your love in all there is.

The End of the Day

God with Me Lying Down

God with me lying down,
God with me rising up,
God with me in each ray of light,
And I have no ray of joy without Him,
    Not one ray without Him.

Christ with me sleeping,
Christ with me waking,
Christ with me watching,
Every day and night,
    Each day and night.

God with me protecting,
The Lord with me directing,
The Spirit with me strengthening,
For ever and for evermore,
    Ever and evermore, Amen.
        Chief of chiefs, Amen.

The Soul Plaint

O Jesus! tonight,
O Shepherd of the poor,
Save me from evil,
Save me from harm,
O save my body,
Sanctify me tonight,
O Jesus! tonight,
Do not leave me.
Endow me with strength,
O Herdsman of might.
Guide me aright,
Guide me in Your strength,
O Jesus! in Your strength
Preserve me.

Sleeping Prayer

I am placing my soul and my body
On Your sanctuary this night, O God,
On Your sanctuary, O Jesus Christ,
On Your sanctuary, O Spirit of perfect truth,
    The Three who would defend my cause,
    And not turn Their backs upon me.

O Creator, who is kind and just,
O Child, who overcame death,
O Holy Spirit of power,
Keep me this night from harm;
    The Three who would justify me
    Keep me this night and always.

The Soul Shrine

God, give charge to Your blessed angels,
    To keep guard around this home tonight,
A band sacred, strong, and steadfast,
    That will shield this soul shrine from harm.

Safeguard, O God, this household tonight,
    Its people, their resources, and their reputations,
Deliver them from death, from distress, from harm,
    From the fruits of envy and of hatred.

Give to us, O God of peace,
    Thankfulness despite our loss,
To obey Your will here below,
    And to enjoy You above.

Bedtime Prayer

O Christ, Child of the Living God,

Bless the four corners of my bed.

Send your angels to smooth the sheets on which I lie,

And tend my mind as I lie down to rest.

Guide my thoughts down quiet paths

So that sleep may come quickly.

Sustainer of the Universe, be my head's pillow.

Shed your light even into my dreams.

May my rest be without hindrance or harm,

And may my waking be holy.

While We Sleep

Bless those minding cattle,
And those minding sheep,
And those fishing the sea,
While the rest of us sleep.

Bless those who tend our roads,
And those who guard our peace,
Bless those who make our food,
While the rest of us sleep.

Bless those who work in hospitals,
And those who bring our mail,
Bless all who toil all night long,
While the rest of us sleep.

Enfolding Your Life in God

God in All Things

God to enfold me,
God to surround me,
God in my speaking,
God in my thinking.

God in my sleeping,
God in my waking,
God in my watching,
God in my hoping.

God in my life,
God in my lips,
God in my soul,
God in my heart.

God in my sufficing,
God in my slumber,
God in my ever-living soul,
God in my eternity.

God in the Everywhere

You are the peace of all things calm.
You are the place to hide from harm.
You are the light that shines in dark.
You are the heart's eternal spark.
You are the door that's open wide.
You are the guest who waits inside.
You are the stranger at the door.
You are the calling of the poor.
You are my Lord and with me still.
You are my love, keep me from ill.
You are the light, the truth, the way.
You are my Savior this very day.

Encircling Prayer

My Christ, my shield, my encircler,
Each day, each night, each light, each dark
My Christ, my Christ! My shield, my encircler,
Each day, each night, each light, each dark,
Be near me, uphold me, my treasure, my triumph,
In my lying, in my standing, in my watching, in my sleeping,
Jesus, Son of David, my strength everlasting!
Jesus, Son of Mary, my helper, my encircler!

Each Thing

Bless to me, O God,
Each thing my eye sees.
Bless to me, O God,
Each sound my ear hears.
Bless to me, O God,
Each odor that goes to my nostrils.
Bless to me, O God,
Each taste that goes to my lips,
Each note that goes to my song,
Each ray of light that guides my way,
Each thing that I pursue,
The passion that drives my living soul,
The Three that seek my heart

Jesus, Son of Mary

Jesus, Son of Mary,
Have mercy upon us,
    Amen.
Jesus, Son of Mary,
Make peace with us,
    Amen.

Oh, with us and for us
Where we shall longest be,
In Your fair Heaven,
     Amen.
Be about the morning of our course,
Be about the closing of our life,
     Amen.
Be at the dawning of our life,
And oh! at the darkening of our day,
     Amen.
Be for us and with us,
Merciful God of all,
     Amen.
Consecrate us
O King of kings,
O God of all,
     Amen.
Each heart and body,
Each day to Yourself,
Each night accordingly,
O King of kings,
O God of all,
     Amen.

Holy Creator of Glory

Thanks be to You, Holy Creator of Glory,
Creator kind, ever-loving, ever-powerful,
Because of all the abundance, favor, and deliverance
That You give us in our need.
Whatever circumstances happen to us as Your children,
In our portion, in our lot, in our path,
Give to us also the rich gifts of Your hand
And the joyous blessing of Your mouth.
Send forth to us the power of Your love,
Leap over the mountains of our transgressions,
And wash us in the true blood of conciliation,
Like the moss of the mountain, like the lily on the lake.

In the steep common path of our calling,
Be it easy or uneasy to our flesh,
Be it bright or dark for us to follow,
Your own perfect guidance be upon us.
Shield us from the wiles of the deceiver,
From the arch-destroyer with his arrows pursuing us,
And in each secret thought our minds do weave,
Stand at our helm and at our sail.

Now to the Creator who made each creature,
Now to the Son who paid ransom for His people,
Now to the Holy Spirit, Comforter of might—

Shield and protect us from every wound.
Be about the beginning and end of our race;
Let us sing in glory,
In peace, in rest, in reconciliation,
Where no tear shall be shed, where death comes no more.
Where no tear shall be shed, where death comes no more.

Blessing of a Restless Heart

Many a time I wish I were other than I am.
I weary of my life's boundaries.
I long to be rid of the weight of my duties.
I hunger for an ampler life.

You, my Savior, who are both wisdom and compassion,
Set me free from the lordship of desire.
Help me to find my happiness here,
In acceptance of my life's circumstance;
In friendly eyes,
In work well done,
In quietness born of trust,
And most of all, in the knowledge of Your presence
Here, in this time, this place.

My Desires

May I speak each day according to Your justice,
Each day may I show Your authority, O God;
May I speak each day according to Your wisdom,
Each day and night may I be at peace with You.

Each day may I count the causes of Your mercy,
May I each day give heed to Your laws;
Each day may I compose for You a song,
May I harp each day Your praise, O God.

May I each day give love to You, Jesu.
Each night may I do the same;
Each day and night, dark and light,
May I praise Your goodness to me, O God.Bless My Life
God, bless the world and all that is therein.
God, bless my spouse and my children,
God, bless the eye that is in my head,
And bless, O God, all that my fingers touch.
What time I rise in the morning early,
What time I lie down late in bed,

  Bless my rising in the morning early,
  And my lying down late in bed.

The Guardian Angel

O angel of God who has charge of me
From the dear Creator of mercy,
Make 'round about me this night
The shepherd's fold of the saints.

Drive from me every temptation and danger,
Surround me on the sea of unrighteousness,
And in the narrows, crooks, and straits,
Keep my small boat, keep it always.

Be a bright flame before me,
Be a guiding star above me,
Be a smooth path below me,
And be a kindly shepherd behind me,
Today, tonight, and forever.

I am tired and I am a stranger,
Lead me to the land of angels;
It is time for me to go home
To the court of Christ, to the peace of Heaven.

Christ's Cross

Christ's cross over this face I wear, and over my ear.

Christ's cross over my eye.

Christ's cross over my nose.

Christ's cross to accompany me before.

Christ's cross to accompany me behind me.

Christ's cross to meet every difficulty both on hollow and hill

Christ's cross eastwards facing me.

Christ's cross back toward the sunset.

In the north, in the south,

Increasingly, may Christ's cross straightway be.

Christ's cross up to broad Heaven.

Christ's cross down to Earth.

Let no evil or hurt come to my body or my soul.

Christ's cross over me as I sit.

Christ's cross over me as I lie.

Christ's cross be all my strength

Until we reach the King of Heaven.

From the top of my head to the end of my toenail,

O Christ, against every danger

I trust in the protection of the cross.

Till the day of my death, when my flesh goes into the clay,

And I shall once more take

Christ's cross over this face.

Prayer of Belief

I believe, O God of all gods,
That You are the eternal Creator of life.
I believe, O God of all gods,
That You are the eternal Creator of love.
I believe, O Lord and God of the peoples,
That You are the Creator of the high heavens,
That You are the Creator of the skies above,
That You are the Creator of the oceans below,
I believe, O Lord and God of the peoples,
That You are the One who created my soul and wove its threads,
Who created my body from dust and from ashes,
Who gave to my body breath and to my soul its possession.
Creator, bless to me my body.
Creator, bless to me my soul.
Creator, bless to me my life.
Creator, bless to me my belief.

When I Am Besieged

Help me, Unity in Trinity,
Trinity in Unity, I beseech you,
For I am in peril.
My mind is besieged by the television,
My heart is trapped by busyness,
And my body grows weak from lack of use.
I ask the high powers of the hosts of heaven
Not to leave me here lost in my life.
Defend me, I pray,
From stress and depression,
Christ, my heart's true love.
Guard me, I ask,
From gossip and unkind words,
Bright God of the High Heavens.
Breathe through me, I beg you, Spirit of God,
That my body may be whole and strong,
And my heart full of your joy.
Help me, Unity in Trinity,
Trinity in Unity, I beseech you.

Journeying

Traveling Blessing

Life be in my speech,
Sense in what I say,
The bloom of cherries on my lips,
Till I come back again.
The love Christ Jesus gave
Be filling every heart for me,
The love Christ Jesus gave
Filling me for every one.
Traversing hills, traversing forests,
Traversing valleys long and wild.
The fair white Mary still uphold me,
The Shepherd Jesus be my shield,
The fair white Mary still uphold me,
The Shepherd Jesus be my shield.

The Ocean Prayer

O Lord, who fills the heavens,
Imprint on us Your gracious blessing,
Carry us over the surface of the sea,
Carry us safely to a haven of peace,
Bless our boatmen and our boat,
Bless our anchors and our oars,

Each stay and rope and traveler,
Our mainsails to our tall masts
Keep, O King of the elements, in their place
That we may return home in peace;
I myself will sit down at the helm,
It is God's own Son who will give me guidance,
As He gave to Columba the mild
That time he set stay to sails.
Mary, Bride, Michael, Paul,
Peter, Gabriel, John of love,
Pour down from above the dew
That which would make our faith to grow,
Establish us in the Rock of rocks,
In every law that love exhibits,
That we may reach the land of glory,
Where peace and love and mercy reign,
All granted to us through grace;
Never shall the canker worm get near us,
We shall there be safe forever,
We shall not be in the bonds of death
Though we are of the seed of Adam.

Prayer for a Journey

Christ walks beside me on this path.
May the land through which I travel be without sorrow.
May the Trinity protect those with whom I stay,
Creator, Child, and Holy Spirit.
Bright angels, journey with me, in every dealing,
That in every dealing no poison may reach me,
That in every dealing Christ's sweetness flows from me.

For Guidance When Lost

God over me, God under me,
God before me, God behind me,
I on Your path, O God,
Knowledge of truth, not knowledge of falsehood,
    That I shall truly see all my quest.
Son of beauteous Mary, King of life,
Give me eyes to see all I search for,
With grace that shall never fail, before me,
    That shall never quench nor dim.

Prayer Before a Car Trip

May the Lord God, Ruler of Heaven and Earth, be our navigator.
May God's Holy Angels guard and protect us as we travel.
May the Saints of God watch over us as we travel.
May the road we travel be smooth and straight,
And safe from all perils.

May each mile we travel bring us ever closer to the Creator.
May each mile we travel bring us ever closer to the Child.
May each mile we travel bring us ever closer to the Holy Spirit.
May each mile we travel bring us ever closer to the Triune God.

In safety and in good fellowship may we travel the road before us!
In safety and in good fellowship may we arrive at our destination!

riving Prayer

O God, defend me as I drive.

May my eyes be sharp,

My hands and feet sure.

Deliver me from all danger on the road.

Let the passengers who ride with me be safe as well.

And protect each person I pass, each hapless beast.

Guard my car with your great shield.

May its tires run smoothly and its engine not fail.

Let each part function as it should.

May no harm come to me and mine as I drive,

And may I do no harm to any other living creature.

Blessings for Children

Blessing for a New Baby

Welcome, small bright one!
We bid you welcome here
On this sweet Earth where we do live.
May the sunshine give you joy,
May the wind fill your heart with tenderness,
May the green trees show you how to lift up your head,
And may the beasts of the Earth teach your hands
To reach out in love.
Welcome, small bright one!
We bid you welcome here,
In the Name of the Three in One.

Prayer While Washing a Baby

May these three palmfuls of waters
Bless you with the Sacred Three.
One palmful of the Creator of life.
One palmful of the Christ of love.
One palmful of the Spirit of peace.
The God of Threefold Love wash you always
And keep you clean.

The Baptism Blessing

O Being who inhabits the heights
Imprint Your blessing quickly,
Remember the child of my body,
In Name of the Creator of peace;
Grant her the blessing of the Three
　　Who fill the heights.
　　The blessing of the Three
　　Who fill the heights.

Sprinkle down upon her Your grace,
Give to her virtue and growth,
Give to her strength and guidance,
Give to her all the possession that she needs,
Sense and reason without deceit,
Angel wisdom in her day,
That she may stand without reproach
　　In Your presence.
　　She may stand without reproach
　　In Your presence.

Mother's Consecration

May the great God be between your two shoulders,
To protect you in your going and in your coming,
May the Son of Mary be near your heart,
And the perfect Spirit upon you pouring—
Oh, the perfect Spirit upon you pouring!

A Mother's Faith-Cry

O Great God, to whom to love and to be are one,
Hear my faith-cry for those who are more Yours than mine.
Give each of them what is best for each.
I cannot tell what it is—but You know.
I only ask that You love them and keep them
With the same loving and keeping
You did show Mary's Child and Yours.

Prayer for a Child Going to School

Go with the kiss of God upon your head.

Go with the arms of Jesus around your shoulders.

Go with the breath of the Spirit on your face.

Mount the steps of the school bus

Your heart filled with peace and courage.

Learning and knowledge are blessed by God—

Remember this.

Friendship and laughter are doubly blessed by God—

Remember this.

Love and compassion are triply blessed by God—

Remember this.

Prayer for a Child's New Clothes

May you wear these new clothes

With safety and laughter

In every place

Your foot does step.

May they clothe you with warmth,

With confidence,

With health,

With love,

With the grace of the Threefold Spirit.

Seeing God in Nature

Jesu Who Ought to Be Praised

There is no plant in the ground
But is full of His virtue,
There is no shape on the seashore
But is full of His blessing.

> Jesu! Jesu! Jesu!
> Jesu! It is right to praise Him.

There is no life in the sea,
There is no creature in the river,
There is nothing in the heavens,
But proclaims His goodness.

> Jesu! Jesu! Jesu!
> Jesu! It is right to praise Him.

There is no bird on the wing,
There is no star in the sky,
There is nothing beneath the sun,
But proclaims His goodness.

> Jesu! Jesu! Jesu!
> Jesu! It is right to praise Him.

The One Who Lights the Stars

Behold the One who lights the stars
On the crests of the clouds,
And the singers of the sky
    Praising You.

Coming down with acclaim
From the Creator above,
Harp and lyre of song
    Sounding to You.

Christ, O refuge of my love,
How can I not add my voice!
Angels and saints together
    Singing to You.

O Son of Mary of the graces,
Of exceeding white purity of beauty,
My joy is to be in the fields
    Of Your riches.

O Christ my beloved,
O Christ of the Holy Blood,
By day and by night
    I praise You.

Deep peace the Earth shall breathe to you,
O weariness, here,
O ache, there!
Deep peace, a soft white dove to you.
Deep peace, a quiet rain to you.
Deep peace, an ebbing wave to you.
Deep peace, red wind of the east to you.
Deep peace, gray wind of the west to you.
Deep peace, dark wind of the north to you.
Deep peace, blue wind of the south to you.
Deep peace, pure red of the flame to you.
Deep peace, pure white of the moon to you.
Deep peace, pure green of the grass to you.
Deep peace, pure brown of the soil to you.
Deep peace, pure silver of the dew to you.
Deep peace, pure blue of the sky to you.
Deep peace, pure gold of the sun to you.
Deep peace of the running wave to you.
Deep peace of the flowing air to you.
Deep peace of the quiet Earth to you.
Deep peace of the sleeping stones to you.
Deep peace of the stars to you.
Deep peace of the Son of Peace to you,
Who shines everywhere in this sweet Earth,
Deep peace, deep peace!

Patrick's Shield

I arise today
Through the strength of Heaven:
Light of sun,
Radiance of moon,
Splendor of fire,
Speed of lightning,
Swiftness of wind,
Depth of sea,
Stability of earth,
Firmness of rock.

Lord of Creation

Let us adore the Lord,
Maker of marvelous works,
Bright heaven with its stars,
The sweet Earth with its green trees,
And the white-waved sea.

The Miracle of Creation

Almighty Creator, it is You who made
The land and the sea.
The world cannot contain
The wonder of the song You sing us,
Even though each blade and leaf should sing aloud
Your wonders, O true Lord!

The Creator made the world,
A miracle too great to express its measure,
Letters cannot describe it, words cannot contain it.
He who made the wonder of the world
Will save us, has saved us.
Nothing is too great a toil for God.

Taliesen's Prayer of Beauty

Beautiful it is that God shall save me.

Beautiful too the bright fish in the lake,

Beautiful too the sun in the sky,

The beauty of an eagle on the shore when the tide is full,

The beauty of desire and the love between lovers,

Beautiful too a gift which is loved,

Beautiful too the moon shining on the Earth,

The beauty of summer, its days long and slow,

The beauty of flowers on fruit trees,

Beautiful the covenant of the Creator with Earth,

The beauty in the wilderness of doe and fawn,

The beauty of wild leeks and the berries of harvest,

The beauty of the heather when it turns purple,

Beautiful the pastureland,

Beautiful too the beasts who suckle their young,

The beauty of water shimmering,

The beauty of the world where the Trinity speaks,

But the loveliest of all is the Christ

Who lives in all beauty.

The Blessings of Light, Rain, and Earth.

May the blessing of light be on you, light without and light within.

May the blessed sunlight shine on you like a great warm fire,

So that stranger and friend may come and warm themselves at it.

And may light shine out of the two eyes of you,

Like a candle set in the window of a house,

Bidding the wanderer come in out of the storm.

And may the blessing of the rain be on you,

May it beat upon your spirit and wash it fair and clean,

And leave there a shining pool where the blue of Heaven shines,

And sometimes a star.

And may the blessing of the Earth be on you,

Soft under your feet as you pass along the roads,

Soft under you as you lie out on it, tired at the end of day;

And may it rest easy over you when, at last, you lie out under it.

May it rest so lightly over you

That your soul may be out from under it quickly,

Up and off and on its way to God.

And now may the Lord bless you always, and bless you kindly.

Filling the Bird Feeder

The chickadee, the jay, the nuthatch, the sparrow,
I welcome all birds to my feeder!

In the Name of the Creator who made you!
In the Name of the Son who loves you!
In the Name of the Spirit who sustains you!

May I be a blessing to you as you are a blessing to me.

Celebrating the Seasons

Blessing of the Seasons

Saints of four seasons, saints of the year,
Loving, I pray to you; longing, I say to you,
Save me from angers, sorrows, and dangers!
Saints of four seasons, saints of the year.

Saints of the green springtime,
Saints of the year,
Patrick and Grighair, Brigid be near.
My last breath gather with God's foster father,
Saints of the green springtime,
Saints of the year.

Saints of gold summer,
Saints of the year,
Poetry gives wings to me, fancy far brings me,
Guide me to Mary's sweet Son
Saints of gold summer,
Saints of the year.

Saints of red autumn,
Saints of the year,
Look! I am cheery, Michael and Mary,
Open wide Heaven to my lonely soul,
Saints of red autumn,
Saints of the year.

Saints of gray winter,
Saints of the year,
Bitter the cold, forsaken my heart,
Guard my soul from despair and defeat,
Saints of gray winter,
Saints of the year.

Saints of four seasons,
Saints of the year,
Waking or sleeping, through my life creeping,
Life in its night still sheds God's light,
Saints of the four seasons,
Saints of the year.

The Blessing of the New Year

God, bless to me the new day,
Never granted to me before;
It is to bless Your presence
You have given me this time, O God.

Bless to me my eyes,
May my eyes bless all they see;
I will bless my neighbor,
May my neighbor bless me.

God, give me a clean heart,
Let me stay in the sight of Your eyes;
Bless to me my children and my spouse,
And bless to me my work and my possessions.

At Imbolc

I thank You, Lord, for the wisdom of the ancestors,
Who marked the coming of spring in bleak February.
For shining-bright Brigid!
For Candlemas Day, when tradition tells us to be sure to have
Half our wood and half our hay.
For the groundhog lumbering out of his den.
For the lengthening day and the higher-arcing sun.
For the drip of the icicle at the eave.
For a spring that starts on a snowy day.
For a spring eternal in the Word of Your beloved Child.

On this day, Your Son the Light of the World
Was presented in the Temple:
Let me rejoice in the coming of light!
On this day, sweet Brigid's eternal flames
Bring new life to the Earth:
May I rejoice in the coming of light!
All praise and all thanksgiving to the God of the Springtime,
As the icicle drips at the eave and the dawn comes ever-earlier!

Maytime Prayer

Maytime is a fair season,
With its bird song and bright trees,
With the plow in the furrow,
While the sea is green
And many colors clothe the Earth.

The gift I ask of this Maytime,
May it not be denied me,
Is peace between myself and God,
Between myself and all I meet,
Between myself and the sweet Earth.
May this Maytime show me the way
To the gate of glory
That leads to Your court, O Christ.

The Beltane Blessing (May 1)

Mary, mother of saints,
Bless our flocks and milking cow;
Let not hate or harm come near us,
Drive from us the ways of the wicked.

Keep your eye every Monday and Tuesday
On the milking cow and the pair of heifers;
Accompany us from hill to sea,
Gather to yourself the sheep and their lambs.

Every Wednesday and Thursday be with them,
Be your gracious hand always about them;
Tend the cows down to their stalls,
Tend the sheep down to their folds!

Every Friday, O Saint, be at their head,
Lead the sheep from the face of the hills,
With their innocent little lambs following them,
Encompass them with God's encompassing.

Every Saturday be likewise with them,
Bring the goats in with their young,
Every kid and goat to the seaside,

And from the rocks on high,
With the green cresses around their summits.

The strength of the Triune be our shield in distress,
The strength of Christ, His peace and His Endurance,
The strength of the Spirit, Physician of health,
And of the precious Creator, the King of Grace.

Bless ourselves and our children,
Bless every one who shall come from our loins,
Bless him whose name we bear,
Bless, O God, her from whose womb we came.

Every holiness, blessing and power,
Be given to us every time and every hour,
In name of the Holy Threefold above,
Creator, Child, and Spirit everlasting.

Be the Cross of Christ to shield us downward,
Be the Cross of Christ to shield us upward,
Be the Cross of Christ to shield us roundward,
Accepting our Beltane blessing from us,
    Accepting our Beltane blessing from us.

Blessing for August 15, Marymas

On the feast day of Mary the fragrant,
Mother of the Shepherd of the flocks,
I cut a handful of the new corn,
I dried it gently in the sun,
I rubbed it sharply from the husk
  Between my palms.

I ground it in a mill on Friday,
I baked it on a piece of sheep-skin,
I toasted it over a fire of rowan,
And I shared it among my people.

I walked with the sun around my house,
In the name of Mary the Mother,
Who promised to preserve me,
Who did preserve me,
And who will preserve me,
In peace, in flocks,
In righteousness of heart,
In labor, in love,
In wisdom, in mercy,
For the sake of Your Passion.

O Christ of grace
Who till the day of my death
Will never forsake me!
    Oh, till the day of my death
    Will never forsake me!

Picking Tomatoes at Lammas-Tide

In the heat and haze of early August, Lord, I praise Your Holy Name,
For this first harvest of tomatoes from my garden.

For the warm, brown earth they have grown from:
I give thanks to the Creator.
For the thundery summer rain that watered them:
I give thanks to the Child.
For the hot summer sun that has ripened the fruit:
I give thanks to the Spirit.

Each deep red globe, gently twisted from under scented leaves,
A small miracle to hold in my own hand.
By Your bounteous grace, O Lord, and the sweat of my brow,
I have partnered with You in this miracle.

All praise to You, God of the green and growing Earth!
All praise to You, God of rain and sun and fruitfulness!
All praise to You, God of my backyard tomato harvest!

Thanksgiving at Samhain

Lord of the changing seasons,
Of harvest time, frost, and hearth fire,
I thank You for this holy time of the turning year.

A hard freeze this All Saint's Day morning.
The russet leaves fall thickly in the still, early light,
Like all the men and women who have ever lived,
They return to the Earth.
I thank You, Lord, for this moment in time,
This moment of clear revelation.

I thank You for the faith of my ancestors, remembered this day,
For Halloween candy, and pumpkin pie,
And the Communion of Saints,
For cozy evenings
And the low-angled sun of a November afternoon.

In the name of the dead, I thank You!
In the name of the living, I thank You!
In the name of those to come, I thank You!

Celebrating Christmas

An Advent Prayer

Lord of the shortening day,
Of the snowflake, the fir tree, and the ice-rimmed lake,
    Be with me in the dark and cold of these four weeks.

The Faith of the prophets who foretold
His coming to a waiting world,
    Be the Faith in me!
The Hope of the holy men and women who longed for
His coming,
    Be the Hope in me!
The Love of His gentle mother
To whom He came in such humility,
    Be the Love in me!

In faith, in hope, in love,
Through these short, cold days of the early winter,
    Sustain me O God as I await Your coming!

Christmas Carol

This night is the eve of the great Nativity,
Born is the Son of Mary the Virgin,
The soles of His feet have reached the earth,

The Son of Glory down from on high,
Heaven and earth glowed to Him,

    All hail! let there be joy!

The peace of earth to Him, the joy of heaven to Him,
Behold His feet have reached the world;
The homage of a King be His, the welcome of a Lamb be His,
King all victorious, Lamb all glorious,
Earth and ocean illumined to Him,

    All hail! let there be joy!

The mountains glowed to Him, the plains shown to Him,
The voice of the waves with the song of the strand,
Announcing to us that Christ is born,
Son of the King of kings from the land of salvation;
Shone the sun on the mountains high to Him,
All hail! let there be joy!

Shone to Him the Earth and Sphere together,
God the Lord has opened a Door;
Son of Mary Virgin, hasten to help me,
O Christ of hope, O Door of joy,
Golden Sun of hill and mountain,

    All hail! Let there be joy!

Hey the Gift, Ho the Gift

Hey the Gift, ho the Gift,
   Hey the Gift, on the living.

Son of the dawn, Son of the clouds,
Son of the planet, Son of the star,
   Hey the Gift, on the living.

Son of the rain, Son of the dew,
Son of the starry vault, Son of the sky,
   Hey the Gift, on the living.

Son of the flame, Son of the light,
Son of the sphere, Son of the globe,
   Hey the Gift, on the living.

Son of the elements, Son of the heavens,
Son of the moon, Son of the sun,
   Hey the Gift, on the living.

Son of Mary of the God-mind,
And the Son of God first of all news,
   Hey the Gift, on the living.

Hey the Gift, ho the Gift,
   Hey the Gift, on the living.

The Gift of Power

I am the Gift, I am the Poor,
I am the Man of this night.

I am the Son of God in the door,
Seeking the gifts.

Son of the moon, Son of the sun,
Great Son of Mary of God-like mind.

A cross on each right shoulder,
I am in the open door.

I see the hills, I see the strand,
I see angels heralding on high.

I see the dove shapely, gracious,
Coming with kindness and friendship to us.

Blessing Death

The Death Blessing

God, omit not this soul from Your covenant,
Carry this soul on Your own arm, O Christ,
King of the City of Heaven,
And since it was Your right, O Christ, to buy the soul,
At the time of the balancing of the beam,
At the time of the bringing in the judgment,
Be this soul now at Your own right hand,
Oh! at Your own right hand.

And let the Holy Michael, king of angels,
Come to meet the soul,
And lead it home
To the heaven of the Son of God.
The Holy Michael, high king of angels,
Come to meet the soul,
And lead it home
To the Heaven of the Son of God.

Guide My Soul

Thanks to You, O God,
Praise to You, O God,
Honor to You, O God,
For all You have given me.

Grant me grace now as I end my living.
Grant me life as death is coming.
Be with me, O God, as breath casts off,
Be with my soul in the high seas.
Guide my soul through the narrows,
When I cross the deep flood,
And bring me safe to my home
With You, O God.

From the Beginning to the End

As You were before,
At my life's beginning,
Be so again
At my journey's end.
As You were there
At my soul's shaping,
Creator, be there as well
At my journey's close.

As You shone before
At the beginning of my life,
Shine again now
At the end of my course.
Now and henceforth,
As You were in my life, be so in my death,
O Son and O Father,
O Spirit of grace!

Blessing for the Soul Going Home

You go home this night
To your home of winter,
To your home of autumn,
Of spring and of summer.
You go home this night to your lasting home,
To your eternal bed, to your sound sleeping,
And your bright waking.

Sleep now, sleep, and so fade sorrow.
Sleep, my beloved, in the rock of the fold.

The sleep of seven lights upon you, my dear.
The sleep of seven joys within you, my dear.
The sleep of seven slumbers upon you, my dear.

Sleep, oh sleep in the quiet of stillness.
Sleep, oh sleep in the way of guidance.
Sleep, oh sleep in the love of all loving.

Blessing at Leave Taking

You are leaving us, going where we cannot go.

God go with you!

Our hearts are breaking to let you go.

Creator carry you!

You leave us bereft and torn.

Holy Child stay close to you!

We watch you fade, like day sinking into night.

Bright Spirit shine on you!

Keep you safe when we no longer see you.

Keep our hearts knit in love when we no longer touch your hand.

Give you songs and laughter

As you enter Heaven's Door,

And dry our tears.

Eternity

Eternal Life

To Christ the seed,
To Christ the harvest,
To the barn of Christ
May we be brought.

To Christ the sea,
To Christ the fish,
In the nets of Christ,
May we be caught.

From birth to age,
From age to death,
Your two arms, Christ,
Will keep us safe.

From death to life,
Not ended but re-grown,
In the fields of Paradise,
May we be sown.

Brigid's Heavenly Banquet

I would like to have the people of Heaven in my house
With vats of good cheer laid out for them!
I would like to have the three Marys, their fame is so great.
I would like people from every corner of Heaven.
I would like them to be cheerful in their drinking.
I would like to have Jesus too here among them.
I would like a great lake of beer for the King of kings.
I would like to be watching Heaven's family
Drinking it through all eternity.

Where I Shall Longest Live

This Earth, with its green hills and white-waved seas,
Is sweet to my heart.
Each beast and flower, each mountain and river,
Tells me that Heaven must be sweeter yet,
For how else could I be happy there,
Where I shall longest live?

Let me see each day, Fair Lord, sweet Three-in-One,
Heaven's golden light
Shining on my work, my home,
My daily food, my loved ones,
And the fair Earth.
Let me live in Eternity
Both now, and forevermore.

Notes on the Prayers

Prayers on pages 73, 89, 95, 100, 101, 104 (top) were written by William Palmer, 2010. Bill is a senior editor at Anamchara Books and an active member of Trinity Episcopal Church in Binghamton, New York. He is proud to have a little Celtic heritage of his own, courtesy of his beloved grandmother, Charlotte Kelly Palmer (who would have been 115 years old this year).

Prayers on pages 18, 23 were written by Zachary Chastain, 2010. Zac grew up in the greater Binghamton area of upstate New York, where he still lives today. He spends most of his free time reading, making music, or acting in one of the local theaters' productions. He works as an editor and staff writer for Anamchara Books.

Prayers on pages 41, 42 (bottom) 47, 79 (top) were written by Sheila Stewart, 2010. Sheila is a senior editor at Anamchara Books. She grew up in Northern Newfoundland, within steps of the Atlantic Ocean and has loved the wild, rocky places ever since. She also loves words. The power of words, with their ability to reflect the beauty and terror of truth, never ceases to amaze her. Today, she lives in Vestal, New York, with her two young children, to whom she wants to impart a sense of wonder, joy, and overwhelming love.

Prayers on pages 26 (bottom), 32 (top), 37, 44, 54, 68, 74, 76 (top), 79 (bottom), 85 (bottom), 114, 118 were written by Ellyn Sanna, 2010. Ellyn is the executive editor of Anamchara Books. The daughter of a Wesleyan minister, she grew up spending most of her free time in the woods. As an adult, these two influences continue to shape her awareness of the world. Over the years, she has written many books in a variety of genres, but she is most excited by the opportunities she has now at Anamchara Books to use words to explore the world's "thin places," creating books that reveal this world's many expressions of the Holy.

Prayers on pages 14, 15, 16–17, 20, 21 (top), 22, 24, 25, 26 (top), 30, 31, 36, 43, 45, 46, 50, 51, 52, 53, 58, 59, 60–61, 62–63, 64, 65, 66, 67, 70, 71, 72, 76 (bottom), 77, 78 (top), 82, 83, 88, 94, 96, 97–98, 99, 104–105, 106, 107, 110, 111, 112, 113, 116 are modern adaptations of prayers found in the *Carmina Gadelica* (Song of the Gaels), a collection of prayers, hymns, charms, and blessings translated from the Gaelic by Alexander Carmichael. Carmichael collected this treasure trove of prayer at the end of the nineteenth century from the Gaelic-speaking crofters and fisher folk of the Highlands and Islands of Scotland. It reflects the oral traditions of more than 1500 years of Celtic Christianity.

Prayers on pages 27, 32 (bottom), 33, 40, 42 (top), 60 (top), 85 (top), 117 are modern adaptations from *Ancient Irish Poetry*, translated by Kuno Meyer and published in 1913.

Prayers on pages 21 (bottom), 55, 84, 86, 87, 92–93 are modern adaptations from *The Poem Book of the Gael*, translated by P.J. McCall and published in 1912.

Prayers on pages 34, 63, 78 (bottom) are modern adaptations from *Hebridean Altars*, a collection of sermons based on prayers from the Scottish people. The author, Alistair MacLean, was a Scottish minister in the early twentieth century (and the father of the thriller author by the same name).